Copyright © Jonathan Lee 2005

Published 2005 by CWR, Waverley Abbey House, Waverley Lane, Farnham, Surrey GU9 8EP England.

The right of Jonathan Lee to be identified as the author and illustrator of this work has been asserted by him in accordance with the Copyright, Designs and Patents Act 1988.

All rights reserved. No part of this publication may be reproduced, stored in a retrieval system, or transmitted, in any form or by any means, electronic, mechanical, photocopying, recording or otherwise, without the prior permission in writing of CWR.

See back of book for list of National Distributors.

Bible verses taken from the Good News Bible copyright © American Bible Society 1966, 1971, 1976, 1992, 1994.

Concept development, editing, design and production by CWR.

Illustrations: Jonathan Lee

Printed in England by Linney Print

ISBN 1-85345-362-5

Remember When Jesus Walked On The Sea

Written and illustrated by Jonathan Lee

It was raining outside and the school day had finished. Mrs Phips had a wonderful story to tell her class of a miracle Jesus performed to rescue His disciples. As the class sat quietly Mrs Phips cleared her throat, 'Uh hem,' and began to read . . .

One night Jesus went up onto a mountain to pray. After being with so many people each day He would often go somewhere alone to pray to His Father in heaven. The disciples, however, were somewhere very different...

They decided to get into a boat to cross the Sea of Galilee. As the night became darker, the wind blew stronger... and stronger still... until eventually...

Jesus, meanwhile, was still on the mountain praying to His Father. But because of His great love and power He could see His disciples struggling in the stormy sea.

So He went to their rescue....

As Jesus came to the edge of the water He could see the mighty waves but He was not afraid. Nothing could stop Him reaching His friends that He loved. He took one step out onto the water and began to walk on the sea...

The disciples were now far away from land and in great danger when suddenly they could see a man coming towards them walking on the sea.

Now they were really terrified and wondered who or what it could be.

As Jesus drew near to the disciples, He spoke through the howling wind and said, 'It's Me. Don't be afraid!'

Peter, the disciple, answered Jesus and said ...

As soon as Jesus pulled Peter out of the water and walked with him back to the boat the wind and the waves became still and calm. Peace was all around.

The disciples, now full of wonder and amazement, worshipped Jesus saying, 'You really are the Son of God!'

Mrs Phips closed the book to look around at her class sitting in quiet wonder. The silence was quickly disturbed by Andrew as he launched his hand into the air and asked . . .

'Well Andrew, we don't really understand how Jesus performed His miracles, but we do know that He is the Son of God.

Through Jesus all things were created, the sky and all that's above it... the earth and all that's on it... the sea and all that's in it...

When Jesus walked on earth He was God with a face. All creation was at His command for He had created all creation,

But when we look to Jesus for help we will find that He is always with us in the storm and will speak His calmness and peace saying, "It's Me, don't be afraid."

feeling unwell
feeling frightened
first day back at school
friends

No matter what happens, where we are or where we go, or how afraid we get...

'... Remember when Jesus walked on the sea.'

Remember When Jesus Walked On The Sea

📖 Psalm 46 v 1 → Help Peter find out more about how God is always with us by filling in the missing [words]...

v1 "God is our ☐ and ☐

always ☐ to ☐ in

☐ of ☐

Titles in this series

Remember The Wise and Foolish Builders
ISBN: 1-85345-303-X

Remember The Good Samaritan
ISBN: 1-85345-301-3

Remember The Lost Sheep
ISBN: 1-85345-302-1

Remember When Jesus Fed 5000 People
ISBN: 1-85345-361-7

Remember When Jesus Healed the Sick
ISBN: 1-85345-363-3

Remember The First Christmas
ISBN: 1-85345-317-X

Remember The First Easter
ISBN: 1-85345-330-7

All books £3.99 each (plus p&p)

Prices correct at time of printing